Military Transformation: Army Actions Needed to Enhance Formation of Future Interim Brigade Combat Teams: GAO-02-442

U.S. Government Accountability Office (GAO)

The BiblioGov Project is an effort to expand awareness of the public documents and records of the U.S. Government via print publications. In broadening the public understanding of government and its work, an enlightened democracy can grow and prosper. Ranging from historic Congressional Bills to the most recent Budget of the United States Government, the BiblioGov Project spans a wealth of government information. These works are now made available through an environmentally friendly, print-on-demand basis, using only what is necessary to meet the required demands of an interested public. We invite you to learn of the records of the U.S. Government, heightening the knowledge and debate that can lead from such publications.

Included are the following Collections:

Budget of The United States Government
Presidential Documents
United States Code
Education Reports from ERIC
GAO Reports
History of Bills
House Rules and Manual
Public and Private Laws

Code of Federal Regulations
Congressional Documents
Economic Indicators
Federal Register
Government Manuals
House Journal
Privacy act Issuances
Statutes at Large

United States General Accounting Office

Report to Congressional Committees

May 2002

MILITARY TRANSFORMATION

Army Actions Needed to Enhance Formation of Future Interim Brigade Combat Teams

GAO-02-442

Contents

Results In Brief	2
Background	4
IBCTS Are Expected to Fill a Perceived Gap in Military Capability	7
Regional Commander in Chiefs View Planned IBCTS Favorably and Could Use Them in Various Ways	13
IBCTs Would Fill a Capabilities Gap	13
Challenges Have Arisen in Forming the Initial IBCT	19
Installation Support Needed for IBCTs Has Been Greater than Anticipated	27
Lessons Learned on Brigade Formation Are Not Readily Available	31
Conclusions	33
Recommendations for Executive Action	34
Agency Comments and Our Evaluation	35
Scope and Methodology	37

Appendixes

Appendix I:	Sections from Public Laws 107-107 and 106-398 Concerning Limitations on Army Transformation Actions	40
Appendix II:	Comments from the Department of Defense	45

Figures

Figure 1:	Examples of Legacy Weapon Systems—Black Hawk Helicopter, Bradley Fighting Vehicle, and Abrams Tank	6
Figure 2:	Representative Interim Armored Vehicles—Mobile Gun System Vehicle and Infantry Carrier Vehicle	9
Figure 3:	C-130 Aircraft	11
Figure 4:	Areas of Operational Responsibility for the Geographical Combatant Commands	16
Figure 5:	Army's Approach to Develop Multi-Skilled Soldiers	22
Figure 6:	A C-17 Aircraft and a C-5A Aircraft That Would Provide Strategic Lift for the IBCT	23
Figure 7:	Comparison of Fiscal Year 2001 Retention Rates for Soldiers in the IBCTs, at Fort Lewis, and throughout Forces Command	26
Figure 8:	Comparison of IBCT and I Corps Soldiers Electing to Remain in Their Existing Unit	27

Contents

Figure 9:	Shoot House Training Facility Constructed at Fort Lewis to Train IBCT Soldiers to Confront the Enemy in an Urban Setting	29

United States General Accounting Office
Washington, D.C. 20548

May 17, 2002

The Honorable Carl Levin
Chairman
The Honorable John W. Warner
Ranking Minority Member
Committee on Armed Services
United States Senate

The Honorable Bob Stump
Chairman
The Honorable Ike Skelton
Ranking Minority Member
Committee on Armed Services
House of Representatives

In October 1999, the U.S. Army announced its intentions to transform its forces into a more strategically responsive force that could more rapidly deploy and effectively operate in all types of military operations, whether small-scale contingencies or major theater wars. Army plans call for an over 30-year transformation that will lead to the ability to deploy a brigade anywhere in the world within 96 hours, a division in 120 hours, and five divisions within 30 days. The first step in this process is to form and equip six Interim Brigade Combat Teams (IBCT) by 2008. The first two brigades are being formed at Fort Lewis, Washington, with the goal of organizing, equipping, training, and certifying the first such brigade to deploy by May 2003. The Army Chief of Staff stated that it would cost approximately $1 billion to form each brigade.

Because these brigades are entirely new, many questions have arisen as to how their capabilities differ from those of more traditional brigades, how the Army plans to use them, and whether they will possess capabilities that the war-fighting Commanders in Chief (CINC) need. Thus, we monitored IBCT formation at Fort Lewis during 2001 to gain a better understanding of the challenges that have arisen that might apply to subsequent brigades scheduled to be formed in other locations. We also visited the war-fighting CINCs responsible for Europe, Southwest Asia, Korea, and the Pacific to gain their perspectives on how they might use these brigades. Our objectives were to (1) identify the expected capabilities of the IBCT, (2) determine the CINCs' views on the utility of the IBCTs and how the CINCs might use them, (3) identify the challenges that have arisen in forming the brigades, and (4) determine if the Army has an effective means of capturing lessons learned. This is the third in a planned series of reports related to Army Transformation and is being provided to you because of your oversight responsibilities for these issues.[1]

Results In Brief

The IBCT—intended to be a lethal and survivable deterrent force that can be rapidly deployed anywhere in the world—was devised to fill a gap in military capability. The Army's heavy combat forces, though lethal and survivable, are not rapidly deployable, and its light infantry forces are rapidly deployable but lack survivability and lethality. Although the IBCT is optimized for use in small-scale contingencies, it is also expected to engage in all types of military conflicts, including a major theater war when supplemented with additional forces and weapons. Its interim vehicles are designed to maneuver in various kinds of terrain, from mountains to urban settings. Its digital systems are intended to allow soldiers to "see" an enhanced view of the battlefield through robust intelligence, reconnaissance, and surveillance. These capabilities are expected to enable the IBCT to engage an enemy before coming into actual contact. The Army will test and validate new doctrine, training, and leadership development concepts as well as new organizational structures in the IBCTs. This is intended to provide insights for future transformation.

The war-fighting CINCs believe that the IBCT's planned capabilities will help fill a gap in capability by providing a rapidly deployable force that is both lethal and survivable. The specific uses that the CINCs envision for the IBCTs vary according to the unique requirements of their respective regions. However, they generally agreed that the IBCTs as envisioned would provide them with a broader choice of capabilities to meet their operational requirements.

The Army faces numerous challenges in forming its first IBCT that need to be addressed. For example, some planned combat capabilities will not be present when the IBCT is to be certified for deployment in May 2003. Specifically, two interim armored vehicles—the mobile gun system vehicle and the nuclear, biological, and chemical vehicle—require further development and will not be delivered until 2004, requiring substitute

---

[1] U.S. General Accounting Office, *Military Transformation: Army Has a Comprehensive Plan for Managing Its Transformation but Faces Major Challenges*, GAO-02-96 (Washington, D.C.: Nov. 16, 2001); *Defense Acquisition: Army Transformation Faces Weapons Systems Challenges* (GAO-01-311, May 21, 2001).

vehicles in their stead. Similarly, training challenges exist since the interim armored vehicle delivery schedule has compressed the time available for training. The IBCT will not have a full 6 months to train after receiving most of the vehicles as desired by Fort Lewis officials. However, a senior Fort Lewis official contended that all the training requirements would be accomplished in the reduced time available. In addition, maintaining proficiency in digital systems has challenged the IBCT due to personnel turnover. As a result, the Training and Doctrine Command is currently developing a plan to sustain soldier skills on the digitized systems for the two brigades. However, the Army has a draft plan for sustaining soldiers' skills on digitized systems that will be applicable to the entire Army. Further, it is questionable whether the Army will be able to deploy its first brigades anywhere in the world in 96 hours. While this is now only a goal for the IBCTs, it is a requirement for units entering the force after 2008. The first IBCTs will likely not meet this goal due to both the lack of a sufficient number of aircraft to meet the timetable and possibly the need for airfield upgrades. Further, the IBCT is designed to carry limited supplies and after 72 hours to "reach" for needed logistical support from, among others, a foreign country's commercial system. However, the Army has not yet determined how this approach will work. The deployability shortfall and combat capability shortfalls create risks for the CINCs to consider. However, information about the extent of these shortfalls has not been made available to the CINCs so they can plan for mitigating any identified risks.

Additional challenges have arisen at Fort Lewis. As a human capital challenge, reenlistment data show that digitally trained soldiers have been transferring out of the IBCT. This disrupts the continuity that is important to these new brigades. The Army has developed a personnel stabilization policy to help retain soldiers and avoid the constant training of new soldiers, but it does not have data to determine why the soldiers left. Such data would enable the Army to decide what actions might be needed to reduce personnel turnover. With respect to IBCT installation support, Fort Lewis has had to assume an increased maintenance workload because the IBCT was designed with fewer maintenance personnel in order to deploy quickly. Fort Lewis officials had to request additional funds to absorb the additional workload. Such a workload increase can be expected at the installations that will be home stations to future IBCTs.

Army officials believe that the organization created at Fort Lewis to help form the brigades has been effective in addressing day-to-day challenges, thereby permitting brigade officials to concentrate on critical training and operational matters. Further, the Army has a process in place that chronicles lessons learned in forming the IBCTs. However, this information is not readily available to the rest of the Army from a central source. By not having that information available for research, the Army may be unaware of previous best practices or repeat mistakes in forming subsequent IBCTs.

We are recommending that the Secretary of Defense direct the Army to provide the CINCs with the combat capability limitations and logistical requirements that the first IBCT will have when it is certified for deployment. This information will assist the CINCs in their planning to mitigate any risks associated with the employment of the IBCT. Because some mobility issues are beyond the Army's purview and a long lead time could be necessary to rectify any identified shortfalls, we are further recommending that the Secretary of Defense obtain the Army's specific IBCT mobility requirements to meet its 96-hour deployment goal and determine how best to address any shortfalls. Additional recommendations are aimed at enhancing future IBCT formation by addressing other challenges that have arisen in forming the first brigade.

In commenting on a draft of this report, the Department generally agreed with the report's findings and recommendations and outlined ongoing management actions to address the concerns named in the report.

Background

In testimony before the U.S. Senate in March 2000,[2] the Chief of Staff of the Army stated that the Army had to transform to meet current and future strategic requirements. The Army believes that the transformation is necessary to respond more effectively to (1) the growing number of peacekeeping operations and small-scale contingencies and (2) the challenges posed by nontraditional threats such as subnational and transnational terrorist groups. The Army plans to transform its forces over a 30-year period.

The first phase of the Army's transformation is to form six IBCTs, the first two of which are being formed at Fort Lewis, Washington. The first of these brigades has been in the process of being formed since fiscal year 2000. The Army's plan is to certify it as achieving its initial operational

---

[2] Testimony before the Committee on Armed Services, U.S. Senate, March 1, 2000.

capability by May 2003, at which time it will be deployable. The second brigade is in its early stages of formation. The Army has programmed funding for six IBCTs and has announced the locations of the remaining four.[3] Under current plans, all six brigades are to have been formed, equipped, trained, and ready to deploy by 2008. The Army is also considering how it might accelerate the fielding of the last three brigades so that all six can be fielded by 2005. Additionally, the 2001 Quadrennial Defense Review stated that an IBCT be stationed in Europe. Because this was not in the Army's plans, it is considering establishing an IBCT in Europe. Taken together, the IBCTs represent what the Army terms its Interim Force because it begins to meet the Army's rapid deployment needs for the next decade.

Beginning in 2008 and continuing beyond 2030, the Army plans to transition to its Objective Force.[4] During this period, all Army forces, including the IBCTs, are to be transformed into new organizational structures operating under new war-fighting doctrine. Their new combat systems are to be lighter and more mobile, deployable, lethal, survivable, and sustainable than current systems. Four competing research and development teams have completed work on alternative designs for these future combat systems and a contract has been awarded to a single lead systems integrator.

As the Army transitions to its Objective Force, it plans to maintain the organizational designs of a portion of its existing combat force, which it terms its Legacy Force, and to modernize selected equipment in this force. This equipment includes such major weapons systems as the Abrams tank, Bradley Fighting Vehicle, and Black Hawk helicopter. Figure 1 depicts these weapons systems. This selective modernization is intended to enable the Army to maintain capability and readiness until the future combat systems are delivered to the Objective Force.

---

[3] The first two are a heavy brigade of the 2nd Infantry Division and a light infantry brigade of the 25th Infantry Division both of which are at Fort Lewis. The next four are the 172nd Infantry Brigade (Separate), Forts Wainwright and Richardson, Alaska; the 2nd Armored Cavalry Regiment (Light), Fort Polk, Louisiana; the 2nd Brigade, 25th Infantry Division (Light), Schofield Barracks, Hawaii; and the 56th Brigade of the 28th Infantry Division (Mechanized), Pennsylvania Army National Guard.

[4] The Objective Force is the force that achieves the objectives of the Army's transformation. This future force will be rapidly deployable and capitalize on advances in science and technology. These advances will enable the Army to equip its forces with significantly advanced systems such as the Future Combat System.

Figure 1: Examples of Legacy Weapon Systems—Black Hawk Helicopter, Bradley Fighting Vehicle, and Abrams Tank

Source: U.S. Army.

IBCTS Are Expected to Fill a Perceived Gap in Military Capability

The Army expects the IBCT to provide a force capability that it does not currently have: a rapidly deployable early-entry combat force that is lethal, survivable, and capable of operating in all types of military operations, from small-scale contingencies like the Balkans' missions to a major theater war. It also expects to use the IBCT to test new concepts that would be integrated into the Army's future Objective Force. Many of these concepts are still under development.

Expected Uses

The IBCT has been optimized for small-scale contingencies, being specifically designed to operate in a variety of terrains, including mountains and urban areas. Yet it is expected to also be capable of participating in a major theater war and addressing both conventional and nonconventional threats. As an early-entry force, the brigade is expected to have sufficient built-in combat power to conduct immediate combat operations upon arrival in theater if required. It is designed to supply its own needs for 72 hours, after which time it would need a source of resupply. The IBCT is intended, in general, to fight as a component of a division or corps but also be capable of operating separately under the direct control of a higher headquarters, such as a joint task force. The Army expects that in many possible contingencies, the IBCT could initially be the single U.S. maneuver component under a higher headquarters.

In a major theater war, the IBCT under current plans would fight as a subordinate maneuver component within a division or corps. However, the brigade would be augmented with additional mission-specific combat capabilities such as armor, aviation, and air defense artillery. The Army, however, is considering the need for an Interim Division structure that would include IBCTs as the maneuver forces because some analyses have concluded that placing an IBCT with its differing design into an existing infantry or armored division might impede the division's ability to achieve its full combat capabilities. The Army expects to complete the new divisional concept by spring 2003 if the Chief of Staff decides to go forward with it.

Expected Organization, Equipment, and Capabilities

The IBCT is organized primarily as a mobile infantry organization and will contain about 3,500 personnel and 890 vehicles. The brigade includes headquarters elements; three infantry battalions, composed of three rifle companies each; an antitank company; an artillery battalion; an engineer company; a brigade support battalion; a military intelligence company; a signal company; and a unique Reconnaissance, Surveillance, and Target Acquisition squadron. This squadron is expected to be the IBCT's primary source of combat information through the traditional role of reconnaissance, surveillance, and target acquisition. However, the squadron is also designed to develop a situational understanding of other elements within the operational environment, including political, cultural, economic, and demographic factors. This awareness is expected to enable the brigade to anticipate, forestall, or overcome threats from the enemy. The squadron offers the IBCT a variety of new systems and capabilities that are generally not contained in an infantry brigade including manned reconnaissance vehicles and ground reconnaissance scouts, counterintelligence, human intelligence collectors, unmanned aerial vehicles, ground sensors, and radars. Moreover, the squadron's all-weather intelligence and surveillance capabilities, coupled with the digitized systems, are designed to enable it to maintain 24-hour operations.

All six of the IBCTs are planned to be equipped with new light-armored wheeled vehicles, termed interim armored vehicles, which are significantly lighter and more transportable than existing tanks and armored vehicles. These vehicles include ten types of vehicles that share a common chassis— infantry carriers, mobile gun systems, reconnaissance and surveillance vehicles, and others. These wheeled vehicles are expected to enable the IBCT to maneuver more easily in a variety of difficult terrains. The first vehicles were scheduled for delivery to the first brigade in April 2002. Meanwhile, the brigade has been training on substitute vehicles, including 32 Canadian infantry vehicles and German infantry carrier and nuclear, biological, and chemical vehicles. These vehicles approximate the capabilities of the interim armored vehicles. Figure 2 depicts two of the interim armored vehicles.

Figure 2: Representative Interim Armored Vehicles—Mobile Gun System Vehicle and Infantry Carrier Vehicle

Source: U.S. Army.

The brigade's digitized communications are designed to enable brigade personnel to "see" the entire battlefield and react before engaging the enemy. In addition to light armored vehicles equipped with digital systems, the IBCT is expected to rely on advanced command, control, computer, communications, intelligence, surveillance, and reconnaissance systems purchased from commercial or government sources. The squadron's all-weather intelligence and surveillance capabilities, together with its digitized systems, are intended to enable it to maintain 24-hour operations. The Army expects this awareness to enable the IBCT to anticipate, forestall, or overcome threats from the enemy.

The IBCT's planned capabilities also differ in other ways from those found in traditional divisional brigades. For example, the Army determined that achieving decisive action while operating in various types of terrain, including urban settings, would require the brigade to possess a combined arms capability at the company level, rather than at the battalion level. Focusing on dismounted assault, companies are expected to support themselves with (1) direct fire from weapon systems on the infantry carrier vehicle and from the mobile gun system and (2) indirect support through mortars and artillery. This combined arms capability is to be reinforced through the Army's current development of a training program aimed at developing soldiers with a wider range of skills as well as leaders who can adapt to many different kinds of conflict situations.

Expected Deployment Capability and Relation to Objective Force

The Army expects the IBCT to rely on new sustainment concepts that will permit it to deploy more rapidly because it will carry fewer supplies and have lighter vehicles, resulting in less weight to be shipped. Due to its smaller and lighter vehicles, the Army expects that the IBCT will be transported within the theater by C-130 aircraft. There are more of these aircraft, and they provide greater access to airstrips than would be possible with larger C-17 and C-5A aircraft that are intended for use in deploying an IBCT from its home station to the theater. Figure 3 shows a C-130 aircraft.

Figure 3: C-130 Aircraft

Source: U.S. Air Force.

The IBCTs will serve an additional purpose in that they will test and validate new doctrine and organizational structures as well as new combat training and leadership development concepts. As such, the Army expects the formation and operation of the IBCT to provide insights for subsequent transformation.

Estimated Schedule for Accelerating IBCTs

In September 2001, Army officials announced the possibility of accelerating the formation of the last three IBCTs. Under this proposal, all six IBCTs would be formed by 2005, 3 years earlier than planned. A key to acceleration is the ability of the manufacturer to deliver the vehicles ahead of the current delivery schedule. According to this schedule, the first IBCT would begin receiving its vehicles in April 2002. The second brigade would begin receiving its vehicles in February 2003.

The Army cannot acquire vehicles for more than the second IBCT until it meets certain legislative requirements.[5] The Army must compare the costs and operational effectiveness of the Interim Armored Vehicle with its existing vehicles before it can acquire the Interim Vehicle for the third IBCT. The Army must also complete an operational evaluation of the first IBCT. The evaluation must include a unit deployment to the evaluation site and execution of combat missions across the spectrum of potential threats and operational scenarios. The Army cannot acquire vehicles for the fourth and subsequent IBCTs until the Secretary of Defense certifies that the operational evaluation results indicate that the IBCT design is operationally effective and suitable. The significance of this is that the Army would need to complete this evaluation and authorize vehicle production for the fourth brigade by June 2003 for the Army to accelerate formation of the fourth and subsequent brigades, as has been proposed. This is because the manufacturer must have 330 days of lead time to produce and deliver the vehicles.

---

[5] See appendix I for the specific legislative requirements that are contained in section 113, Floyd D. Spence National Defense Authorization Act for Fiscal Year 2001, P. L.106-398 (Oct. 30, 2000) and section 113, National Defense Authorization Act for Fiscal Year 2002, P. L. 107-107 (Dec. 28, 2001).

Regional Commander in Chiefs View Planned IBCTS Favorably and Could Use Them in Various Ways

Our visits to the unified combat commands covering Europe, Southwest Asia, the Pacific, and the United Nations Command/U.S. Forces in Korea confirmed their support for the Army's plans for the IBCT. They generally agree that the current Army force structure does not meet their requirements for a rapidly deployable, lethal, and survivable force. According to the CINCs, if the IBCTs are formed and deployable as planned, they should fill the perceived near-term gap in military capability. The CINCs view the IBCT as a means to provide them with a broader choice of capabilities to meet their varied operational requirements rather than a substitute for current force structure. However, CINC planners need information about the brigade's deployability and other limitations for planning purposes. Their anticipated uses of an IBCT vary from serving as an early entry force within the European Command to conducting reconnaissance and securing main supply routes in Southwest Asia for the Central Command. To ensure that the CINCs' needs and concerns are addressed as the transformation evolves, the Army has created a forum that meets periodically with their active participation.

IBCTs Would Fill a Capabilities Gap

Our discussions with CINC officials confirmed their agreement with Army conclusions about a gap in military capability. In announcing the Army's plans for its transformation in October 1999, the Army's Chief of Staff pointed to this gap in current war-fighting capabilities and the IBCT's planned ability to rapidly deploy. He noted that although the Army can dominate in all types of conflicts, it is not strategically responsive. The light forces can deploy within a matter of days but lack combat power, tactical mobility, and the ability to maintain sustained operations. On the other hand, armor and mechanized forces possess significant combat power and are able to maintain sustained operations but cannot deploy rapidly.

CINC officials cited past military operations that pointed to this gap. For example, in the Persian Gulf War, the Army deployed a light infantry force—the 82nd Airborne Division—as the early entry force to deter Iraq and defend Saudi Arabia. However, there is general agreement that this force did not possess the anti-armor capability to survive and stop a heavy armored attack. Moreover, it took 6 months to position the heavy forces and associated support units and supplies needed to mount offensive actions against Iraq—a time frame that might not be available in the future. The urban operation in Mogadishu, Somalia, in October 1993 that resulted in the deaths of 16 U.S. soldiers was also mentioned to illustrate the need for a force that is lethal, is maneuverable, and provides sufficient protection to U.S. forces. The difficulty in maneuvering heavy vehicles in peacekeeping operations in the Balkans was also cited by CINC representatives as a reason why lighter, more maneuverable vehicles are needed.

CINC officials pointed out many features of the IBCT that they felt would address the existing capability shortfalls. These features included its planned ability to deploy within 96 hours anywhere in the world and to provide a formidable, survivable deterrent force that could bring combat power to bear immediately if necessary. Also mentioned was its expected ability to rapidly transition from being a deterrence, to serving in a small-scale contingency, to fighting in a major theater of war in the event operations escalated.

CINC officials also commented on the IBCT's enhanced capabilities for situational awareness. Situational awareness is the ability to see and understand the battlefield before coming into actual contact with the opponent through the use of advanced integrated systems that provide command, control, communications, computer, intelligence, surveillance, and reconnaissance capabilities. This expected improvement in awareness should provide a major comparative advantage over potential enemies. They also noted that the IBCT would support their rapid deployment needs by using interim armored vehicles that would be deployable within theater by C-130 aircraft, which are more readily available, better able to access small airfields, and therefore better able to be moved around the battlefield. CINC officials also pointed out that the IBCT relies on a family of vehicles with a common platform, which reduces logistics and support requirements through commonality of spare parts, fuel, and lubricants.

While generally positive about the IBCTs, CINC officials cautioned that many questions remain about whether these brigades will be able to achieve all their envisioned capabilities, especially by the time they are certified for deployment. Concerns expressed to us included

- whether the IBCT would actually be available to deploy anywhere in the world in 96 hours, given many potential competing demands for mobility assets;

- what combat capability shortfalls might exist in the IBCT until it receives all its planned vehicles and weapon systems;

- whether new logistics concepts would succeed in reducing supply tonnages sufficiently to achieve rapid deployment and intratheater goals;

- when the vehicles that need further development, such as the mobile gun system and the nuclear, biological, and chemical vehicle, would be available; and

- whether the IBCT will be able to provide sufficient combat power when heavy forces are needed.

CINC operational and logistics planners need specific data regarding the brigade's combat capabilities and logistics factors that are not yet available. They emphasized that it was important to have these data to adequately integrate the IBCTs into their plans. If, for instance, certain planned capabilities would not be in place when the first IBCTs become deployable, planners would need to know this so that they could plan for mitigating any risks that this might create. For example, Army officials in Korea related their concern that the IBCT will not include the mobile gun system until after the Army certifies the brigade as operationally capable. In the Korean theater, the capability of this weapon system is a high priority.

CINC officials raised additional concerns about the IBCT's support on our visits. Logistics planners in Korea said the amounts of fuel, water, and ammunition used by the brigade need to be analyzed to determine what the theater needs to have when a brigade arrives. Although Korea contains significant support resources, logistics planners need to know the unit's unique and specific support requirements. In the Pacific Command, questions remain regarding the adequacy of the IBCT's 3-day supply of medical items.

CINCs' Employment of IBCTs Will Vary

The CINCs' specific requirements and planned use for the IBCTs varies depending on the requirements of their respective areas of operational responsibility. (See fig. 4.) Officials in both Europe and Korea expressed their views that IBCTs could be used effectively in their theaters of operation. Officials of the U.S. Central Command, which covers Southwest Asia, said that an IBCT had utility in their theater—notably Africa—where fighting in urban terrain might occur. According to Pacific Command officials, their theater could use Army forces that are more deployable, lethal, and sustainable than currently assigned, especially for use in the urban areas prevalent in that theater. CINC representatives generally did not expect the IBCT to substitute for forces currently assigned. Rather, they saw the IBCT as providing them with a broader choice of capabilities to meet their operational needs.

Figure 4: Areas of Operational Responsibility for the Geographical Combatant Commands

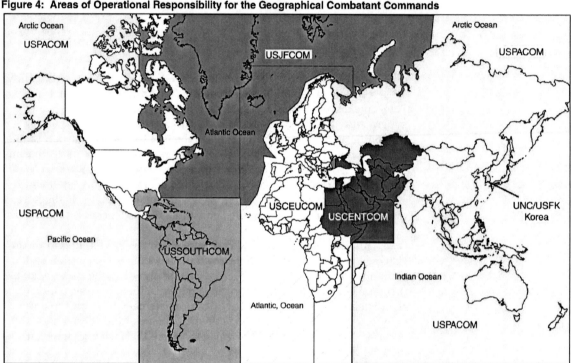

Source: U.S. Army.

Legend:

USEUCOM – U.S. European Command
USCENTCOM – U.S. Central Command
USPACOM – U.S. Pacific Command
UNC/USFK – United Nations Command/U.S. Forces Korea

U.S. European Command

The European Command wants the Army to station an IBCT in its area of responsibility. As noted earlier, the most recent Quadrennial Defense Review stated that an IBCT would be stationed in Europe. Command officials emphasized that the planned characteristics of the IBCT—rapid deployment, enhanced situational awareness, tactical mobility, and lethality—are key to the requirements of the European theater. Further, the expected intelligence-gathering capabilities of the IBCT reconnaissance squadron will exceed that of the Command's currently assigned divisions. This capability is a necessity for missions such as those in the Balkans.

Recognizing strategic and tactical mobility deficiencies from past and ongoing contingency operations in the Balkans, in the year 2000 Command officials in fact created a rapid reaction force with some of the same characteristics as the IBCT. This rapid reaction force is composed of both light and heavy forces and is expected to deploy within 24 hours after being alerted. By using on-hand forces and equipment, the European Command has created an immediate reaction force that possesses some of the IBCT's capabilities. However, this reaction force lacks the intelligence, reconnaissance, and surveillance systems found in the IBCT that allows greater situational understanding of the battlefield. Furthermore, the force is not equipped with the new interim armored vehicles, which allows for a commonality among sustainment requirements and training. Command officials said that an IBCT would complement this rapid reaction force by providing an early entry force that could bring more combat power to bear.

U.S. Central Command

The Central Command's primary area of responsibility is Southwest Asia and is one of two geographic areas that have required war planning for a major theater war. One official noted that an IBCT could provide significant capability to the CINC's theater engagement plans by providing mobile training teams and other military-to-military missions with developing nations.

Command officials stated that the IBCTs would offer new capabilities to their theater in certain circumstances. For example, had an IBCT been available during the Persian Gulf War, the IBCT could have been used rather than the 82nd Airborne Division since the IBCT's planned anti-armor capability far exceeds that of a light division. Moreover, the IBCT would be useful in conducting missions such as reconnaissance and security and securing main supply routes. Command officials stated that an IBCT would have been valuable had it been available for the urban mission in Mogadishu, Somalia, during October 1993. They added that the IBCT could also be used for evacuating noncombatants. Command officials noted that even though the IBCT offers them new capabilities, they would not substitute it for the heavy combat forces that are required for a major war such as the Gulf War.

United Nations Command/ U.S. Forces Korea	Army officials in Korea have stated that they want to station an IBCT in Korea. According to one senior Army official in Korea, the IBCT would provide the maneuverability and combat power needed to operate in the mountains and the increasingly urbanized areas of Korea. War planners in Korea expressed their view that the IBCT is optimized to meet the operational requirements of the Korean peninsula and that the IBCT would have more utility than Bradley Fighting Vehicles and M1 tanks. They explained that these latter weapons would have to be used primarily as stationary weapon platforms because the terrain and the sprawling urban terrain limit their use. They noted that IBCTs are more mobile than light forces and once equipped with all their new weapon systems will have good lethality and be survivable. Further, according to CINC officials, the theater will not lose or diminish its combat capability by substituting IBCTs for heavy forces.
U.S. Pacific Command	While Pacific Command officials noted that Army forces currently assigned to the theater are capable of meeting most CINC operational requirements, an IBCT would bring certain desirable capabilities to the theater. For example, an IBCT would provide increased situational awareness, tactical mobility, and firepower currently unavailable within assigned Army forces. Command war planners explained that the IBCT's communications capabilities would help eliminate some communications shortfalls between and among the Command's service components. Moreover, an IBCT could be more effectively employed for stability and support operations in the Pacific, providing a rapid deployment capability. They mentioned that the planned capabilities of the IBCT offer both (1) considerable flexibility by having substantial nonlethal capabilities for use in stability and support missions and (2) substantial lethality for more intense operations such as peace enforcement. Command officials noted that the IBCT's interim armored vehicles would provide better protection for infantry forces than can be provided by currently assigned infantry forces.

Forum Exists to Address CINC Concerns

The Army has established a CINC Requirements Task Force that provides a forum for the commanders to voice their current and future requirements. Army officials assigned to the combatant commands stated that the quarterly meetings have allowed the CINCs to ensure that their concerns are heard. Issues raised are then forwarded to the Army staff for resolution. For example, the task force has addressed issues such as how the U.S. Pacific Command plans to employ IBCTs in that theater as well as reintegrating the Army's first IBCT into the operational plans. Based on discussions with combatant command officials, the perceived value of the forum is such that participation at the quarterly meetings is generally obligatory for command representatives.

Challenges Have Arisen in Forming the Initial IBCT

Fort Lewis officials said that they are generally satisfied with the progress being made to date in fielding the first IBCT and believe the IBCT is on track to meet its certification milestone of May 2003. However, the Army has encountered challenges in forming the IBCT at Fort Lewis. One challenge to overcome is a combat capability shortfall in the first IBCT when it is certified. Specifically, certain specialized interim vehicles, such as the mobile gun system, will not be available. Further, the interim armored vehicle delivery schedule has compressed the time available for soldiers to train on the vehicles; personnel turnover resulted in more time spent on digital training than planned; and the 96-hour deployment capability, while a goal rather than a requirement, will not be attained by the first IBCT. Army planners are still developing plans on how the IBCT will obtain needed logistics support in the theater after its planned 72-hour supply is depleted. Other challenges relate more to the first IBCT; its home station, Fort Lewis; and potentially, future home stations. These challenges include retention of skilled soldiers and the increased costs to provide maintenance support and facilities at Fort Lewis and ultimately to subsequent IBCT home stations.

First IBCT Will Not Possess All Envisioned Combat Capabilities

Delivery Schedule for Interim Armored Vehicles Will Impact Planned Combat Capabilities at Certification Date

The first IBCT will not achieve all designed combat capabilities by the time it reaches its certification date because it will not have all the interim infantry vehicle variants. One key variant it will lack is the mobile gun system, which is expected to be more capable than the system currently being used. Until the first IBCT is fully equipped with its complement of interim armored vehicles, it will be limited in its designed capabilities by using in-lieu-of vehicles. Specifically, until the mobile gun system vehicle and the nuclear, biological, and chemical vehicle arrive, the IBCT cannot fully meet its planned war-fighting capabilities. These vehicles—particularly the mobile gun system—are critical to meet the expectations of the war-fighting CINC in Korea, as well as the Army's transformation plans. Based on the current delivery schedule, at the time of its operational certification in May 2003, the first IBCT will have about 86 percent of its interim armored vehicles and the remaining 14 percent will be approved substitutes. Army regulations allow a unit to use substitute equipment and vehicles to meet its initial operational capability date. The first mobile gun systems and nuclear, biological, and chemical vehicles will be delivered beginning in 2004.

Delayed Vehicles and Digitized Systems Have Created Training Challenges

The Army has encountered training challenges due to the delivery schedule for the interim armored vehicles and the need for extensive training on digital systems. Despite these challenges, training officials believe that the IBCT has made great strides in achieving training goals, including the transformation goal of developing soldiers who are skilled in a wide range of tasks so that they can transition quickly from small-scale contingencies to higher levels of combat and the reverse.

Because deliveries of the interim vehicles are not scheduled to begin until April 2002, the IBCT has been dependent on substitute wheeled infantry carriers loaned by the Canadian and German governments. These vehicles have been passed from unit to unit, thereby limiting training to company level and below. Training officials said that although they were disappointed that they did not have sufficient vehicles to train as a battalion or brigade, a hidden benefit was that the IBCT was able to focus more training on individual and dismounted infantry skills instead. According to a senior Fort Lewis official, subsequent brigades should not experience the same training limitations as the first brigade unless, for any unforeseen reason, the contractor's expected delivery schedule cannot be met. However, the first brigade will experience a further training challenge in that the revised delivery schedule will compress the time available to train at the battalion and brigade level to just 3 months. Fort Lewis training officials would have liked to have a full 6 months to train after receiving most of the vehicles. However, a senior Fort Lewis official also told us that he is confident that all the training requirements will be accomplished in the lesser time available.

The need to train IBCT soldiers in digital systems has posed other challenges. Digitization provides a critical situational awareness capability to the IBCT similar to that afforded units at Fort Hood, Texas, under the Army's Force XXI program.[6] These systems use sophisticated information

---

[6] This Army initiative begun, in the mid-1990s, involved equipping infantry troops at Fort Hood, Texas, with digitized equipment and testing it in several field exercises. The IBCT is being equipped with these same digitized systems.

technology, that allows personnel in the IBCT to achieve superior battlefield information enabling them to engage the enemy long before coming into contact. IBCT soldiers train with many digitized systems and must maintain specific levels of proficiency. Maintaining proficiency in these systems has been challenging due to personnel turnover in the IBCT. The Army does not currently have a formal digital sustainment-training program for individual soldiers and leaders. Fort Lewis officials cited their concerns that without a digital sustainment-training program, soldier skills will quickly erode. The Army Training and Doctrine Command is currently developing an individual digital sustainment-training program for the two brigades, which may be applicable to the entire Army. However, the Army has not yet implemented initial formal training in digitized systems within its institutional centers and schools; as a result, many individual leaders and soldiers arrive at the IBCT unit without any prior experience with the hardware or software. The Army plans to begin teaching digitized systems at its schoolhouses in 2004, but even then, the training will only be an initial overview.

As part of the Army's multi-skilled soldier concept, the Army's Infantry branch has combined the occupational skill specialties of infantryman, fighting-vehicle infantryman, and heavy anti-armor weapons infantryman into a single consolidated specialty and will train them in a wide range of infantry skills. Army officials spoke favorably about this concept and said that concerns that the Army may be requiring too many skills and capabilities for individual soldiers to absorb have not been borne out in their experience so far. In their view, individual soldiers at Fort Lewis had adapted well to the requirements of the digitized systems and multiple combat skills needed for IBCT missions. They are generally satisfied with the progress being made to date and believe that the IBCT is on track to meet its certification milestone of May 2003. Figure 5 depicts a schematic of this multi-skilled soldier approach.

Figure 5: Army's Approach to Develop Multi-Skilled Soldiers

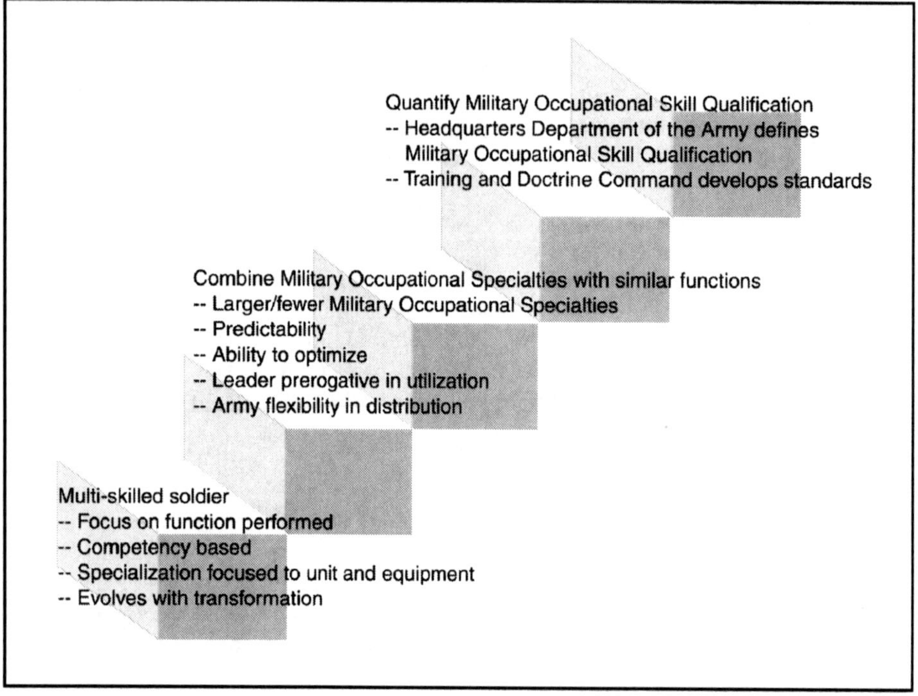

Quantify Military Occupational Skill Qualification
-- Headquarters Department of the Army defines Military Occupational Skill Qualification
-- Training and Doctrine Command develops standards

Combine Military Occupational Specialties with similar functions
-- Larger/fewer Military Occupational Specialties
-- Predictability
-- Ability to optimize
-- Leader prerogative in utilization
-- Army flexibility in distribution

Multi-skilled soldier
-- Focus on function performed
-- Competency based
-- Specialization focused to unit and equipment
-- Evolves with transformation

Source: U.S. Army.

Impediments to Achieving Deployability Goals

The Army's ability to meet its rapid deployment goal for the first IBCT will depend on availability of aircraft to transport unit equipment, completed infrastructure improvements at Fort Lewis specifically, and Air Force certification of the IBCT as deployable. In commenting on the draft report, Army officials stated that Air Force certification of the interim armored vehicle is currently underway with weight and load certification scheduled for May 2002.

Initially the Army announced that the IBCTs would be capable of deploying within 96 hours anywhere in the world, but the Army has since made it a goal for the IBCTs rather than a requirement. It has not established a substitute deployability timetable for the first IBCT. However, under current plans, the Army retains the 96-hour deployment requirement for the future transformed units entering the Army's force following formation of all six brigades in 2008. Other requirements for this future force are to be able to deploy a division in 120 hours and five divisions in 30 days.

It appears that this 96-hour deployability goal for the first IBCT will not be achieved. Army transportation planners have determined that it would take 201 C-17 and 51 C-5 aircraft to transport all of the IBCT's equipment to a distant theater. (See fig. 6.) Army officials have stated that with all the competing demands for these aircraft, the Air Force currently does not possess sufficient numbers of them to meet the 96-hour goal for the IBCTs. Additional analyses would be needed to evaluate other ways to supplement this capability, such as through the forward positioning of some materials or the use of commercial aircraft. Strategic airlift is an Air Force responsibility and therefore beyond the purview of the Army.

Figure 6: A C-17 Aircraft and a C-5A Aircraft That Would Provide Strategic Lift for the IBCT

Source: U.S. Air Force.

The installation where an IBCT is located will dictate the additional infrastructure requirements necessary to deploy the brigade. In October 2000, the Army's Military Traffic Management Command reported in its Army Transformation study that the existing infrastructure at Fort Lewis and McChord Air Force Base could not meet the Army's requirements for deploying the IBCT. The study identified five projects at the air base and Fort Lewis that needed to be constructed or upgraded at an estimated cost of about $52 million. Since the publication of the report, the Army has funded four of the five projects at a cost of more than $48 million and begun one of the projects. The remaining project requires improvements to deployment ramps at McChord Air Force Base. According to Army officials, the remaining project has not been funded and will most likely not be completed before the Army certifies the IBCT as deployable in May 2003.

Another impediment to achieving this goal is the Air Force's certification that the IBCT and all its equipment items can be loaded on and deployed by aircraft. The Air Force cannot certify the unit until the vehicles are fielded and loaded aboard the aircraft in accordance with combat mission requirements. The fiscal year 2002 National Defense Authorization Act requires the Secretary of the Army to conduct an operational evaluation of the first IBCT and the Secretary of Defense to certify that its design is operationally suitable and effective. The evaluation is to include deployment of the brigade to the site of the evaluation. Generally, the IBCT cannot be deployed outside the United States until this requirement is met.[7] A successful evaluation will be necessary if the Army is to achieve its goal of having six IBCTs by 2008.

Other Challenges Have Arisen at Fort Lewis

Personnel Stabilization Has Been the Key Human Capital Challenge

Army officials recognized early on that some form of personnel stabilization policy for the IBCTs might be needed to provide sufficient continuity of leadership and training to the brigade. However, the delay in setting up the policy and certain exemptions from the policy have led to more turbulence than officials would have liked. They believe that the personnel turnover may have diminished training effectiveness in some instances and may have led to devoting more time than they could afford to digitization training.

Officials explained that the need for stabilization stems from the unique nature of the training being done at Fort Lewis and from the normal Army rotational policy that generally has personnel rotating between assignments in 2 years or less. In short, when the trained personnel rotate out of the IBCT, they take their training with them; but no equally trained personnel are available to rotate in. Consequently, the IBCT requires a constant program of providing basic training to incoming personnel on digital equipment, which is available only at Fort Lewis or Fort Hood.

---

[7] The law permits the Secretary of Defense to waive this limitation if deployment is required by national security interests.

Moreover, because this skill is perishable, periodic refresher training is also required. Similarly, the IBCT is training to future war-fighting concepts and doctrine and new concepts for leadership development. Finally, the first IBCT expects to begin receiving some of its interim armored vehicles, which are not available elsewhere in the Army. These unique training requirements argue for more continuity than can be achieved through the normal Army rotational policies that create a constant turnover of personnel within a 24-month period.

Recognizing this need for more continuity, Fort Lewis officials expressed to Army headquarters their concern that permitting normal policies to remain in place would adversely affect the IBCT's readiness and ability to achieve certification on time. In response, the Department of the Army established a formal stabilization policy for the IBCTs in May 2001. Except for certain exemptions under this policy, soldiers must remain in an IBCT for 1 year following certification of the brigade's operational capability.

By stabilizing its soldiers, the unit had hoped to reduce the amount of time it has to spend on training soldiers new to the IBCT on digital and other specialized equipment. Unfortunately, the stabilization policy has not been as effective as officials had hoped. First, the stabilization policy was not in place until May 2001, and by then, many IBCT soldiers had already begun leaving the unit under normal Army rotational procedures. As a result, IBCT trainers spent much of the year repeating their training to new soldiers.

A second problem in the stabilization policy's effectiveness stemmed from the exemptions that are allowed under the policy. For example, soldiers are allowed to rotate out of an IBCT to attend a required school, when promoted, or they can elect to leave an IBCT when they come up for reenlistment. Fort Lewis officials have been encouraged by the fact that IBCT soldiers re-enlisted in fiscal year 2001 at higher rates than those achieved by either of the brigade's higher headquarters—I Corps at Fort Lewis and Forces Command (FORSCOM). As shown by figure 7, all three organizations achieved over 100 percent of the retention goals set by the Army.

Figure 7: Comparison of Fiscal Year 2001 Retention Rates for Soldiers in the IBCTs, at Fort Lewis, and throughout Forces Command

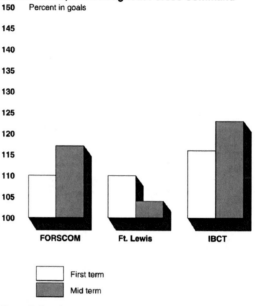

Percent of goal

Legend:
First term=initial term of service of 3 years or less.
Mid term=a subsequent period of 10 years or less.
Source: GAO.

Officials noted, however, that IBCT soldiers who have elected to remain in the Army have not necessarily elected to remain in the IBCT. As shown by figure 8, whereas 34 percent on average of I Corps soldiers elected to remain in their units, only 27 percent of IBCT soldiers elected to stay with the IBCT. Moreover, despite the acknowledged need for continuity in the IBCTs, officials have not been capturing data on the reasons why IBCT soldiers are re-enlisting to leave the brigade early and therefore lack information that could help them reduce personnel turbulence. Further, data are not available to determine which re-enlistment options IBCT soldiers are choosing other than remaining in the unit.

Figure 8: Comparison of IBCT and I Corps Soldiers Electing to Remain in Their Existing Unit

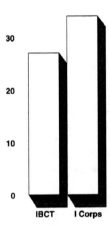

Source: GAO.

Fort Lewis officials said that the problems with stabilization may not be as severe with subsequent brigades since the stabilization policy will be in effect from the beginning, unlike the first brigade when the policy was not instituted until months after its formation began. As a result, Army officials anticipate that these latter brigades will experience fewer departures. Personnel turbulence related to reenlistments would become more significant if the brigades experience slippage in their certification dates and lose more soldiers to re-enlistment transfers.

Installation Support Needed for IBCTs Has Been Greater than Anticipated

The Army specifically designed the IBCT to have fewer support personnel, fewer supplies, and lighter vehicles so that the brigade could be quickly deployed. As a result, the IBCT cannot provide all its own support and requires installation support when located at its home station and other outside support after 72 hours once deployed. In addition, the home station must provide additional and costly facilities for that support.

The IBCT is designed with an austere support battalion that contains fewer mechanics to support and maintain its vehicles. IBCT battalion commanders pointed out, however, that the number of vehicles to support has remained the same, even though the number of mechanics has been reduced by two-thirds. Therefore, the IBCT is capable of conducting only about one-third of its vehicle maintenance requirements. As a result, the IBCT must depend on its home installation for scheduled maintenance support. Fort Lewis addressed this capability limitation by hiring contractors and temporary employees to meet the IBCT support requirements. Fort Lewis officials estimate the IBCT's recurring maintenance requirements at about $11.1 million a year.

After being deployed for 72 hours, the IBCT must be supported by other organizations due to its streamlined support battalion and, under transformation concepts, must "reach" for this support. Under the reach concept, the IBCT is expected to request fuel, ammunition, food, spare parts, water, and other supplies through an integrated distribution system by a linked communications network that includes the IBCT home station, contractor support, and multinational or foreign national commercial systems. Army logistics planners have not yet determined how all this will work. Further, in the interim, the support battalion logistical systems are not yet integrated and lack a dedicated secure network interface to the Army's computerized Battle Command System. As a result, IBCT soldiers are being temporarily used as couriers to relay logistics data between headquarters. The Army's immediate solution to this challenge may be to increase the IBCT support battalion personnel. For the long term, the Army is developing a system software fix.

Providing support to IBCTs will require Army installations to provide new and costly facilities to meet IBCT requirements. The extent and cost of needed improvements at the other installations will vary widely depending upon the location. Army planners noted that it takes at least 3 to 5 years to plan and construct maintenance and other needed infrastructure facilities and that therefore it will be important to develop these plans as soon as possible. Moreover, Army officials have determined that at a minimum, future IBCT home stations will require a mission-support training facility,[8] a fixed tactical Internet, ammunition igloos, and digital classrooms. Examples of long-term requirements include live-fire ranges, maneuver-training areas, mock villages for urban training, and deployment facilities. Figure 9 shows the facility constructed at Fort Lewis to train soldiers in urban warfare techniques.

---

[8] A mission support training facility provides a comprehensive environment within which the IBCT can conduct individual and multi-echelon digital training and mission support.

Figure 9: Shoot House Training Facility Constructed at Fort Lewis to Train IBCT Soldiers to Confront the Enemy in an Urban Setting

Source: U.S. Army.

At Fort Lewis and Yakima Training Center, existing support facilities—such as barracks, motor pools, ammunition storage facilities, and training ranges—need to be upgraded or constructed. To meet IBCT training needs, Fort Lewis converted an existing building to a mission-support training facility, which accelerated the normal new construction timeline. However, all support requirements have not yet been funded. For example, Fort Lewis has requested about $10 million for IBCT communication infrastructure requirements that include a secure fiber optic upgrade to link to McChord Air Force Base. Installations also need the ability to integrate digitized systems between home stations and training centers.

Brigade Coordination Cell Has Proven to Be Valuable Coordinating Mechanism

After the Army announced its planned transformation, the Army Chief of Staff designated the U.S. Training and Doctrine Command as the lead agent for transformation. The Command in turn established the Brigade Coordination Cell (BCC) at Fort Lewis. Its mission is to ensure successful formation of the first two IBCTs at Fort Lewis, synchronize efforts between FORSCOM and the Training and Doctrine Command, and provide insight on Army Battle Command System architecture. The BCC is empowered to directly coordinate with other Army major commands and agencies. It provides a centralized link between the IBCT and a variety of Army organizations responsible for doctrine, training, organization, material, and leadership development. Fort Lewis officials emphasized to us that resolving some of the challenges they are facing points to the need for subsequent installations to establish some sort of mechanism, such as a Brigade Coordination Cell, to deal with the many issues that will inevitably arise.

The BCC is designed as a matrix organization and conduit for feedback between various Army organizations pertaining to training, equipment, and logistics. IBCT soldiers as well as analysts from the BCC, the Army Test and Evaluation Command, and the Center for Army Lessons Learned evaluate and validate training doctrine provided by the Infantry and Armor schools. After training exercises, IBCT commanders and soldiers as well as the appropriate Army agencies provide informal and formal lessons-learned data to the cell. The BCC communicates these data to the doctrine writers for their use as they develop the training support packages for squad-to brigade-level collective tasks and formulate conceptual guidance for use by the IBCT commanders. Cell personnel are a part of the working groups created to solve issues in training, deployment, and logistics. A representative from the Army Materiel Command coordinates the vehicle fielding and its associated new equipment training between the IBCT and the civilian contractors.

The BCC supplements an existing staff hierarchy. It provides staff enforcement and support for the I Corps staff while existing external to the Fort Lewis chain of command. The BCC is not a higher headquarters staff for the IBCT. The cell's focus is the same as its mission—to successfully deliver the first two IBCTs to the Army.

Senior Fort Lewis officials have stated that the BCC has proven to be a valuable means of coordinating activities related to brigade formation and has offered several important benefits. For example, they noted that some of the difficulties that have arisen have been time-consuming to resolve. The existence of the BCC has relieved such burdens from brigade operations personnel so that they could concentrate more on their substantive work, such as training. The BCC also acted as a communication intermediary between the IBCT and the institutional schoolhouses to develop training doctrine for the brigade's new mission requirements. In addition, the BCC relieved Fort Lewis from some of the public affairs requirements. The acknowledged benefits of the BCC have led Fort Lewis officials to conclude that a similar organization may be needed at subsequent locations.

Lessons Learned on Brigade Formation Are Not Readily Available

In accordance with Army regulations,[9] the Army routinely documents the lessons it learns from battles, projects, and reorganizations using memorandums, after-action reports, messages, briefings, and other historical documents. Various organizations traditionally chronicle Army strengths and weaknesses with respect to organization, peacekeeping missions, and wartime operations. During our review, we determined that while fielding the initial IBCT at Fort Lewis, the Army learned valuable lessons that would be critical to future IBCT formation. These lessons were captured and communicated in a variety of ways. However, they were not always forwarded to the Center for Army Lessons Learned, as required, for retention. Further, there is no central location or database where all relevant IBCT lessons learned are available for research. Without having the lessons learned available, the Army may repeat mistakes in fielding subsequent brigades and may lose opportunities that could help it field subsequent brigades more efficiently.

Lessons Learned Not Always Forwarded as Required

Army Regulation 11-33 designates the Center for Army Lessons Learned as the focal point for its lessons-learned system. The regulation stresses that all Army entities are to forward appropriate analytical data, including after-action reports, to the Center. After-action reviews are structured

---

[9] Army Regulation 11-33: Army Lessons Learned Program: System Development and Application, 10 October 1989; Army Regulation 870-5: Military History: Responsibilities, Policies, and Procedures, 29 January 1999.

discussions among commanders and soldiers after military exercises to determine what went right or wrong and what can be improved. However, it appears that the Army is not taking full advantage of this repository to capture all relevant IBCT lessons learned. For example, we found that organizations that have played important roles in the initial brigades' formation are all independently chronicling IBCT fielding information. Furthermore, there is an indication that all lessons learned are not being forwarded to the Center. For example, in May 2001, the Army Test and Evaluation Command published two independent reports that assessed IBCT training events at the squad and platoon levels at Fort Lewis. These reports contained analyses and lessons-learned data about training exercises, equipment, and tasks. The Test and Evaluation Command reports stated that the after-action reviews identified significant issues in conducting adequate equipment training. However, the reports are available from the Test and Evaluation Command, not the Center for Army Lessons Learned.

The Center for Army Lessons Learned published one newsletter dated July 2001 that identified some lessons learned and issues concerning the IBCT. This information was compiled from subject matter experts' observations during training events such as the Senior Leader and Tactical Leaders Course, digital equipment training, and news articles printed in professional publications. Center officials stated that as a result of the terrorist attacks that occurred on September 11, 2001, homeland security has become the Center's primary focus, not the IBCTs. Although the Center intends to publish a second newsletter addressing the support concepts and requirements for the IBCT, it does not anticipate publishing it until later in 2002. An official at the Center for Army Lessons Learned said that information comes in sporadically from disparate sources. Although fielding of the IBCTs is no longer a Center priority, it intends to continue collecting lessons learned and historical information regarding the fielding of the IBCTs and to publish subsequent newsletters as appropriate.

Fort Lewis Held Conference to Share Lessons Learned

Officials at Fort Lewis, at the behest of FORSCOM, hosted an Information Exchange Conference, from November 27 to November 29, 2001, to provide a forum to communicate IBCT lessons learned to officials who will be overseeing formation of subsequent IBCTs as well as to officials from organizations such as Army headquarters, U.S. Army Europe, U.S. Army Pacific, and the National Guard Bureau. At this conference, Fort Lewis officials noted the challenges that they had faced in several areas. The problem areas included personnel turnover and stabilization, digitization training, classroom shortages, issues related to maintenance and support, budget shortfalls related to vehicle maintenance, difficulties related to equipment turn-in, and deficiencies in installation infrastructure. Other lessons learned concerned information technology requirements and the need to establish working relationships throughout the Army. Fort Lewis officials told us that they hoped that the conference attendees would use these lessons learned as they plan and budget for the subsequent brigades at their locations starting in fiscal years 2004 and beyond.

However, it did not appear that these valuable lessons learned would necessarily be readily available for future use. We were told, for example, that FORSCOM would maintain copies of the various slide presentations given at the conference on its Web site for about 12 days. Moreover, there was no plan to submit this information to the Center for Army Lessons Learned for later availability to interested officials of subsequent brigades. While Army officials emphasized that lessons learned are being discussed at all levels throughout the Army, one official commented that he was waiting for the Center for Army Lessons Learned to contact him regarding the lessons identified by his department rather than being proactive about forwarding the information to the Center. Senior officials at Fort Lewis did not know of any other central repository for such information. In our opinion, with the frequent turnover of personnel in the brigades and in some installation functions, it would be valuable to have all IBCT lessons learned available in a central repository.

Conclusions

Successful formation of the first IBCT is critical to the Army's transformation plan because it will begin to fill a near-term gap in military capability and test new concepts that would be integrated into the future Objective Force. Although Army officials are pleased with the progress made thus far, concerns remain about whether all capabilities envisioned for the brigade will be achieved in time for the IBCT's May 2003 certification milestone. Concerns include, notably, the unavailability of the mobile gun system, which provides a key combat capability, and the likelihood that the IBCT will be unable to meet the 96-hour deployment goal due to insufficient quantities of aircraft. Because the IBCT could be deployed to their theaters, it is important that CINC war planners know as soon as possible what planned capabilities are likely to be missing when the brigade is certified as having achieved its initial operating capability. Similarly, logistics planners will need logistics data soon to enable them to plan how best to meet the support requirements of the IBCT if it is deployed to their theater.

Certain challenges have also arisen in forming the first IBCT at Fort Lewis. These challenges include concerns about retaining skilled personnel in the brigade, the ability of IBCT soldiers to sustain their skills on digital systems, and the need for and cost of facility improvements to support the formation of this brigade and, potentially, subsequent brigades. Taking actions now to address these and other challenges faced by the Fort Lewis facility could enhance the chances that subsequent IBCT formations will be accomplished smoothly.

The BCC set up at Fort Lewis appears to have been an effective means of funneling the day-to-day challenges that have arisen in forming the IBCT to the appropriate Army entity for resolution and thus allowing brigade officials to focus on critical training and operational matters. Each installation will likely experience similar issues and benefit from a similar organization. The experiences of those forming the first IBCT and of Fort Lewis in hosting the IBCT provide examples of pitfalls and best practices that, if systematically recorded and made available in a central repository to others throughout the Army, could help the Army form subsequent brigades more efficiently. The Army's Center for Lessons Learned is the designated focal point for lessons learned; however, the Center is neither collecting nor receiving all the lessons learned from forming the first IBCT.

Recommendations for Executive Action

To ensure that regional CINCs have the information they need to plan for mitigating any risks associated with shortfalls in IBCT combat capability as well as logistical requirements, we recommend that the Secretary of Defense direct the Secretary of the Army to

- estimate the combat capabilities that will exist at the time the IBCTs are certified as deployable and set milestones for providing this information to CINC planners and

- provide CINC planners with relevant logistics information as soon as possible so that they can adequately plan how best to support the IBCTs.

Because some mobility issues are beyond the Army's purview and a long lead time could be necessary to rectify any identified shortfalls, we are further recommending that the Secretary of Defense obtain the Army's specific IBCT mobility requirements to meet its goal for deploying a brigade anywhere in the world in 96 hours and determine how best to address any shortfalls.

To assist subsequent installations where IBCTs will be formed in their planning, we recommend that the Secretary of Defense direct the Secretary of the Army to

- expedite development of a program to sustain personnel skills on digitized equipment so that it will be available for subsequent IBCTs,

- collect and analyze data on why soldiers leave the IBCTs and take appropriate action to reduce personnel turnover,

- estimate the extent and cost of facility improvements that will be needed at installations scheduled to accommodate the subsequent IBCTs to assist them in their planning,

- establish a BCC-type organization at subsequent IBCT locations to deal with day-to-day challenges, and

- provide a central collection point for IBCT lessons learned so as to make the information available to personnel throughout the Army.

Agency Comments and Our Evaluation

In commenting on a draft of this report, the Department of Defense generally agreed with the report's findings and recommendations and outlined ongoing management actions to address the concerns noted in the report. In addition, we obtained technical comments from the Department on a draft of this report and incorporated them where appropriate.

In responding to our recommendations that the Army estimate the combat capabilities and logistics requirements of the IBCT and provide the data to CINC planners, the Department acknowledged that since the first IBCT has not been fully fielded, there might be some planning information shortfalls that may inhibit CINC war planning. However, the Department noted that the Army, through the CINC Requirements Task Force, has provided a successful forum to address CINC concerns and derive solutions. We acknowledge that the CINC Requirements Task Force meetings provide a valuable communication tool. Nevertheless, during our fieldwork, CINC operational and logistics planners, who have been represented at these meetings, expressed concerns about not yet receiving specifics regarding the combat capabilities of the IBCT and its logistics requirements. As noted in our report, the planners emphasized that it was important to have these data to adequately integrate the IBCTs into their plans. Moreover, if certain planned capabilities would not be in place when the first IBCTs become deployable, the planners would need to know this. Accordingly, we do not believe that the CINCs' participation in the Requirements Task Force can substitute for being directly provided data on planned combat capabilities and logistics requirements, as we recommended. Providing information as soon as possible to the CINCs would enable operational planners to begin their risk mitigation process in developing their contingency and operational plans.

Regarding Army mobility requirements for the IBCTs, the Department stated that the Army would continue to define the mobility requirements to meet the goals for IBCT deployment. We recognize that prioritization and allocation of lift assets is an operational challenge to be faced by the CINCs and acknowledge that timely allocation of strategic and tactical mobility is needed for the IBCTs to meet planned operational capabilities. However, because the Army does not control mobility allocations, we believe that our recommendation is appropriately directed to the Secretary of Defense, who is in a better position to assess how best to mitigate any projected shortfalls.

With respect to our recommendation that the Army expedite development of a program to sustain personnel skills on digitized equipment that will be available for subsequent IBCTs, the Department said that its ability to accelerate digitized training at the proponent schools was limited due to the equipment delivery schedules. Our recommendation, however, was directed at accelerating development of a sustainment training program for future use at the IBCT locations rather than the proponent schools, as noted in our report. During our review, Army officials expressed concerns that the individual soldiers' digitization skills would quickly erode without a continuing focused regimen of training. Therefore, we continue to believe that the Army needs to expedite developing such a program and implement it as a part of each IBCT's training program.

In responding to our recommendation regarding IBCT reassignments, the Department said that the Army is carefully managing IBCT personnel reassignments pointing to the IBCT personnel stabilization policy that the Army instituted. Although this policy is intended to limit personnel turnover in the IBCT, the fact remains that IBCT soldiers are re-enlisting to leave the IBCT at a higher rate than other units in I Corps. We believe that collecting information on the reasons why IBCT soldiers are leaving at this higher rate would help Army officials identify actions that they might take to encourage re-enlistments in the IBCT. We also believe that this recommendation is especially important in that continuity is critical to achieving training objectives.

In responding to our recommendation concerning facility requirements at subsequent IBCT locations, the Department stated that the Army routinely conducts estimates as part of the annual budgetary process. The Department said that the Army now has a draft transformation template for Army installations that will provide facility requirements to support IBCT stationing, training, and sustainment. The draft template is designed to provide installation planners a starting point to determine their installation peculiar requirements to support an IBCT.

With regard to establishing a BCC-like organization at future IBCT sites, the Department stated that the Army has identified certain functions, processes, and support capabilities required to transform a unit into an IBCT. The Department noted that each IBCT location will have different levels of internal staff capability to execute transformation and that the Army will tailor, on a case-by-case basis, the resources required to fill the shortfalls at each location. We did not intend to dictate the size nor organizational structure for the BCC-like organization we recommended. We agree that as the Army learns about fielding IBCTs, requirements will differ from location to location and the Army should tailor whatever organization it sets up to fit the situational needs.

In response to our recommendation regarding establishing a central collection point for IBCT lessons learned, the Department acknowledged that some lessons learned have not been disseminated throughout the Army nor sent to the Army's Center for Lessons Learned. It said that the Army is planning to establish a central repository and procedures to inform the Army about past and future lessons learned from the Army's transformation as we recommended.

Appendix II contains the full text of the Department's comments.

Scope and Methodology

To identify and gain an understanding of the anticipated capabilities of the IBCT, we discussed planned IBCT capabilities with Army officials at Fort Lewis, Washington; I Corps; the Brigade Coordination Cell; 3rd Brigade/2nd Infantry Division; and officials at the Armor and Infantry Schools and the Combined Arms Center at Fort Leavenworth, Kansas. We also obtained and reviewed various briefing documents, the IBCT Organizational and Operational Concept, the Center for Lesson Learned newsletter, test and evaluation reports, and the IBCT's modified table of organization and equipment.

To determine whether the CINCs believe the IBCTs' planned combat capabilities will meet their requirements, we received briefings and discussed IBCT capabilities with commanders and staff at the U.S. Pacific Command and U.S. Army, Pacific, Honolulu, Hawaii; U.S. Forces Korea and 8th U.S. Army, Seoul, Korea; U.S. European Command, Stuttgart, Germany; and U.S. Army Europe, Heidelberg, Germany; and U.S. Central Command, MacDill Air Force Base, Florida. We reviewed documents that the Army developed concerning its respective areas of responsibility and planning.

To identify challenges in forming the IBCTs, we concentrated our efforts on the first brigade being formed at Fort Lewis since the second brigade is in its early stages of formation. We attended weekly transformation update meetings at Fort Lewis from April 2001 through January 2002 to gain a sense of the challenges being faced. We interviewed the Commanding General and Deputy Commanding General for I Corps and Fort Lewis, the Deputy Commanding General for Training and Readiness, the Deputy Commanding General for Transformation (TRADOC) at Fort Lewis, their staffs, representatives from the Brigade Coordination Cell, the IBCT Commander and his battalion commanders, and the Army Materiel Command's Director of Transformation Support on the extent of issues and challenges that had arisen in forming the first IBCT. In addition, to gain the perspective of the Army's schools for training the IBCTs, we interviewed Army representatives from the U.S. Army Infantry Center, Fort Benning, Georgia; the U.S. Army Armor Center, Fort Knox, Kentucky; and the Combined Arms Center, Fort Leavenworth, Kansas. We obtained and reviewed IBCT training doctrine and manuals and discussed the IBCTs with senior Army officials and their staff to understand IBCT training issues. Based on the results from the Army's weekly IBCT meetings and our interviews and analysis of documentation, we were able to discuss issues regarding potential challenges in the core areas of manning, equipping, training, supporting, and deploying the initial IBCT.

To determine if the Army had an effective means for capturing lessons learned that may be applied to subsequent brigade formations, we interviewed I Corps and Fort Lewis representatives and the BCC historian; received briefings and interviewed representatives from the Center for Army Lessons Learned, Fort Leavenworth, Kansas; and attended the Information Exchange Conference held at Fort Lewis. We obtained reports published by the Center for Army Lessons Learned and the Army's Test and

Evaluation Command with regards to fielding the IBCTs at Fort Lewis. In addition, we acquired the current history files from the I Corps and Fort Lewis historian as well as the regulations for recording the Army's history and lessons learned. As a result, we identified the Army's process to capture lessons learned that may be applied to subsequent IBCT formations.

Our review was performed from April 2001 to March 2002 in accordance with generally accepted government audit standards.

We are sending copies of this report to the Secretary of Defense and the Director, Office of Management and Budget. We will also make copies available to appropriate congressional committees and to other interested parties on request. In addition, the report will be available at no cost on the GAO Web site at http://www.gao.gov. If you or your staff have any questions about this report, please call me at (202) 512-5140.

Major contributors to this report were Reginald L. Furr, Jr.; Beverly G. Burke; Timothy A. Burke; Kevin Handley, M. Jane Hunt; Tim R. Schindler; Pat L. Seaton; and Leo B. Sullivan.

Carol R. Schuster

Carol R. Schuster
Director, Defense Capabilities
 and Management

Appendix I
Sections from Public Laws 107-107 and 106-398 Concerning Limitations on Army Transformation Actions

PUBLIC LAW 107-107—DEC. 28, 2001

SEC. 113. LIMITATIONS ON ACQUISITION OF INTERIM ARMORED VEHICLES AND DEPLOYMENT OF INTERIM BRIGADE COMBAT TEAMS.

Section 113 of the Floyd D. Spence National Defense Authorization Act for Fiscal Year 2001 (as enacted into law by Public Law 106-398; 114 Stat. 165A-23) is amended—

(1) by redesignating subsection (f) as subsection (j); and

(2) by inserting after subsection (e) the following new subsections:

"(f) WAIVER OF COMPARISON REQUIREMENT.—The Secretary of Defense may waive subsections (c) and (e)(1) and submit to the congressional defense committees a certification under subsection (e)(2) without regard to the requirement in that subsection for the completion of a comparison of costs and operational effectiveness if the Secretary includes in the submittal a certification of each of the following:

"(1) That the results of executed tests and existing analyses are sufficient for making a meaningful comparison of the costs and operational effectiveness of the interim armored vehicles referred to in subparagraph (A) of subsection (c)(1) and the medium armored vehicles referred to in subparagraph (B) of such subsection.

"(2) That the conduct of a comparative evaluation of those vehicles in a realistic field environment would provide no significant additional data relevant to that comparison.

"(3) That the Secretary has evaluated the existing data on cost and operational effectiveness of those vehicles and, taking that data into consideration, approves the obligation of funds for the acquisition of additional interim armored vehicles.

"(4) That sufficient resources will be requested in the future-years defense program to fully fund the Army's requirements for interim brigade combat teams.

"(5) That the force structure resulting from the establishment of the interim brigade combat teams and the subsequent achievement of operational capability by those teams will not diminish the combat power of the Army.

"(g) EXPERIMENTATION PROGRAM.—The Secretary of the Army shall develop and provide resources for an experimentation program that will—

"(1) provide information as to the design of the objective force; and

**Appendix I
Sections from Public Laws 107-107 and 106-398 Concerning Limitations on Army Transformation Actions**

"(2) include a formal linkage of the interim brigade combat teams to that experimentation.

"(h) OPERATIONAL EVALUATION.—(1) The Secretary of the Army shall conduct an operational evaluation of the initial interim brigade combat team. The evaluation shall include deployment of the team to the evaluation site and team execution of combat missions across the full spectrum of potential threats and operational scenarios.

"(2) The operational evaluation under paragraph (1) may not be conducted until the plan for such evaluation is approved by the Director of Operational Test and Evaluation of the Department of Defense.

"(i) LIMITATION ON PROCUREMENT OF INTERIM ARMORED VEHICLES AND DEPLOYMENT OF IBCTs.—(1) The actions described in paragraph (2) may not be taken until the date that is 30 days after the date on which the Secretary of Defense—

"(A) submits to Congress a report on the operational evaluation carried out under subsection (h); and

"(B) certifies to Congress that the results of that operational evaluation indicate that the design for the interim brigade combat team is operationally effective and operationally suitable.

"(2) The limitation in paragraph (1) applies to the following actions:

"(A) Procurement of interim armored vehicles in addition to those necessary for equipping the first three interim brigade combat teams.

"(B) Deployment of any interim brigade combat team outside the United States.

"(3) The Secretary of Defense may waive the applicability of paragraph (1) to a deployment described in paragraph (2)(B) if the Secretary—

"(A) determines that the deployment is in the national security interests of the United States; and

"(B) submits to Congress, in writing, a notification of the waiver together with a discussion of the reasons for the waiver.".

Appendix I
Sections from Public Laws 107-107 and 106-398 Concerning Limitations on Army Transformation Actions

PUBLIC LAW 106-398—Oct. 30, 2000

SEC. 113. REPORTS AND LIMITATIONS RELATING TO ARMY TRANSFORMATION.

(a) SECRETARY OF THE ARMY REPORT ON OBJECTIVE FORCE DEVELOPMENT PROCESS.—The Secretary of the Army shall submit to the congressional defense committees a report on the process for developing the objective force in the transformation of the Army. The report shall include the following:

(1) The operational environments envisioned for the objective force.

(2) The threat assumptions on which research and development efforts for transformation of the Army into the objective force are based.

(3) The potential operational and organizational concepts for the objective force.

(4) The operational requirements anticipated for the operational requirements document of the objective force.

(5) The anticipated schedule of Army transformation activities through fiscal year 2012, together with—

(A) the projected funding requirements through that fiscal year for research and development activities and procurement activities related to transition to the objective force; and

(B) a summary of the anticipated investments of the Defense Advanced Research Projects Agency in programs designed to lead to the fielding of future combat systems for the objective force.

(6) A proposed plan for the comparison referred to in subsection (c).

If any of the information required by paragraphs (1) through (5) is not available at the time the report is submitted, the Secretary shall include in the report the anticipated schedule for the availability of that information.

(b) SECRETARY OF DEFENSE REPORT ON OBJECTIVE FORCE DEVELOPMENT PROCESS.—Not later than March 1, 2001, the Secretary of Defense shall submit to the congressional defense committees a report on the process for developing the objective force in the transformation of the Army. The report shall include the following.

(1) The joint warfighting requirements that will be supported by the fielding of the objective force, together with a description of the adjustments that are planned to be made in the war plans of the commanders of the unified combatant commands in relation to the fielding of the objective force.

(2) The changes in lift requirements that may result from the establishment and fielding of the combat brigades of the objective force.

**Appendix I
Sections from Public Laws 107-107 and 106-398 Concerning Limitations on Army Transformation Actions**

(3) The evaluation process that will be used to support decisionmaking on the course of the Army transformation, including a description of the operational evaluations and experimentation that will be used to validate the operational requirements for the operational requirements document of the objective force.

If any of the information required by paragraphs (1) through (3) is not available at the time the report is submitted, the Secretary shall include in the report the anticipated schedule for the availability of that information.

(c) COSTS AND EFFECTIVENESS OF MEDIUM ARMORED COMBAT VEHICLES FOR THE INTERIM BRIGADE COMBAT TEAMS.—(1) The Secretary of the Army shall develop a plan for comparing—

(A) the costs and operational effectiveness of the infantry carrier variant of the interim armored vehicles selected for the infantry battalions of the interim brigade combat teams; and

(B) the costs and operational effectiveness of the troop-carrying medium armored vehicles currently in the Army inventory for the use of infantry battalions.

(2) The Secretary of the Army may not carry out the comparison described in paragraph (1) until the Director of Operational Test and Evaluation of the Department of Defense approves the plan for that comparison developed under that paragraph.

(d) LIMITATION PENDING RECEIPT OF SECRETARY OF THE ARMY REPORT.—Not more than 80 percent of the amount appropriated for fiscal year 2001 for the procurement of armored vehicles in the family of new medium armored vehicles may be obligated until—

(1) the Secretary of the Army submits to the congressional defense committees the report required under subsection (a); and

(2) a period of 30 days has elapsed from the date of the submittal of such report.

(e) LIMITATION PENDING COMPARISON AND CERTIFICATION.—No funds appropriated or otherwise made available to the Department of the Army for any fiscal year may be obligated for acquisition of medium armored combat vehicles to equip a third interim brigade combat team until—

(1) the plan for a comparison of costs and operational effectiveness developed under subsection (c)(1), as approved under subsection (c)(2), is carried out;

(2) the Secretary of Defense submits to the congressional defense committees, after the completion of the comparison referred to in paragraph (1), a certification that—

(A) the Secretary approves of the obligation of funds for that purpose; and

(B) the force structure resulting from the acquisition and subsequent operational capability of interim brigade combat teams will not diminish the combat power of the Army; and

(3) a period of 30 days has elapsed from the date of the certification under paragraph (2).

(f) DEFINITIONS.—In this section:

(1) The term "transformation", with respect to the Army, means the actions being undertaken to transform the Army, as it is constituted in terms of organization, equipment, and doctrine in 2000, into the objective force.

**Appendix I
Sections from Public Laws 107-107 and 106-398 Concerning Limitations on Army Transformation Actions**

(2) The term "objective force" means the Army that has the organizational structure, the most advanced equipment that early twenty-first century science and technology can provide, and the appropriate doctrine to ensure that the Army is responsive, deployable, agile, versatile, lethal, survivable, and sustainable for the full spectrum of the operations anticipated to be required of the Army during the early years of the twenty-first century following 2010.

(3) The term "interim brigade combat team" means an Army brigade that is designated by the Secretary of the Army as a brigade combat team and is reorganized and equipped with currently available equipment in a configuration that effectuates an evolutionary advancement toward transformation of the Army to the objective force.

Appendix II
Comments from the Department of Defense

OFFICE OF THE UNDER SECRETARY OF DEFENSE
3000 DEFENSE PENTAGON
WASHINGTON, DC 20301-3000

ACQUISITION,
TECHNOLOGY
AND LOGISTICS

03 MAY 2002

Ms. Carol R. Schuster
Director, Defense Capabilities and Management
U.S. General Accounting Office
Washington, D.C. 20548

Dear Ms. Schuster:

This is the Department of Defense (DoD) response to the GAO Draft Report, GAO-02-442, "MILITARY TRANSFORMATION: Army Actions Needed to Enhance Formation of Future Interim Brigade Combat Teams," March 28, 2002 (GAO Code 350064). The DoD generally agrees with the report, as noted in the enclosed comments to the GAO recommendations. However, ongoing management actions are appropriate to address the concerns raised in the report, so additional intervention by the Secretary of Defense is not required.

As a result of meetings with the Army staff and continuing visits to the field, the GAO has identified challenges the Army faces during its Transformation. We intend to continue to address these challenges as we attempt to maintain our current timelines for the Army's Interim Force, and will continue to share the results of our efforts with the GAO as it continues its study of the Army's Transformation.

The Department appreciates the opportunity to review the draft report.

Sincerely,

Spiros G. Pallas
Acting Director
Strategic and Tactical Systems

Enclosure

Appendix II
Comments from the Department of Defense

GAO CODE 350064/GAO-02-442

"MILITARY TRANSFORMATION: ARMY ACTIONS NEEDED TO ENHANCE FORMATION OF FUTURE INTERIM BRIGADE COMBAT TEAMS"

DEPARTMENT OF DEFENSE COMMENTS
TO THE RECOMMENDATIONS

RECOMMENDATION 1: The General Accounting Office (GAO) recommended that the Secretary of Defense direct the Secretary of the Army to estimate the combat capabilities that will exist at the time the Interim Brigade Combat Teams (**IBCT**) are certified as deployable and set milestones for providing this information to CINC planners.

DoD RESPONSE: Partially concur. While the report finds the regional CINCs in agreement on the need of an IBCT force with a wide spectrum of capabilities, the GAO report asserted that there exists a lack of information required for CINC planners to fully integrate an IBCT in their war plans. Since the Army has not completed the fielding of the first IBCT and has some materiel challenges to be resolved, there may be planning information shortfalls that may inhibit a CINC's war plans. However, the Army, through the CINC's Requirements Task Force (CRTF), has provided a successful forum to address CINC concerns and derive solutions. As doctrine is finalized and additional collective training is completed, this Task Force will continue to assist CINC planners in the employment of IBCTs. Accordingly, no further direction to the Army is necessary.

RECOMMENDATION 2: The GAO recommended that the Secretary of Defense direct the Secretary of the Army to provide CINC planners with relevant logistics information as soon as possible so that they can adequately plan how best to support the IBCTs.

DoD RESPONSE: Partially concur. The Army has analyzed and approved initial baseline consumption estimates for the IBCT and will ensure CINC planners receive relevant logistics information as soon as possible. The CRTF forum will be utilized to assist as the disseminator of planning information. The Army Service Component Commands will also be provided IBCT sustainment planning guidance. As the Army continues to develop the sustainment doctrine for the IBCT, the Army will ensure it is provided to the CINCs. No further direction to the Army is necessary.

RECOMMENDATION 3: The GAO recommended that the Secretary of Defense obtain the Army's specific IBCT mobility requirements to meet its goal for deploying a brigade anywhere in the world in 96 hours and determine how best to address any shortfalls.

DoD RESPONSE: Partially concur. The Army will continue to define the mobility requirements to meet the goals for IBCT deployment. Prioritization and allocation of lift assets is always likely to be an operational challenge to be faced by the warfighting Commanders in Chief, and IBCT deployment

Appendix II
Comments from the Department of Defense

timelines will be one of many considerations in addressing this challenge. Timely availability of lift is required to fully realize the potential operational capabilities presented by the IBCT.

RECOMMENDATION 4: The GAO recommended that the Secretary of Defense direct the Secretary of the Army to expedite development of a program to sustain personnel skills on digitized equipment so that it will be available for subsequent IBCTs.

DoD RESPONSE: Partially concur. The Army training developers are designing a digital skills sustainment program based on feedback from the Brigade Coordination Cell (BCC) and interaction with the initial Brigade Combat Teams. One of the reasons formal training on digitized equipment cannot accelerate is the acquisition process that delivers the equipment to the proponent schools after Milestone B. The Army should stay on course with the Training and Doctrine Command's development of the Digital Training Strategy scheduled for a May 02 completion date. All training is included in the Institutional Digital Education Plan (IDEP) funded for FY03 through FY09. **Request change to recommendation from "expedite" to read "complete."**

RECOMMENDATION 5: The GAO recommended that the Secretary of Defense direct the Secretary of the Army to collect and analyze data on why soldiers leave the IBCTs and take appropriate action to reduce personnel turnover.

DoD RESPONSE: Partially concur. IBCT personnel reassignments are carefully managed and tracked by the Army's Personnel Command career branches, the Distribution Division, and the losing organizations. To reduce turbulence, soldiers are stabilized in IBCT units from date of arrival until one year after the unit reaches its Initial Operating Capability (IOC). Accordingly, no further direction to the Army is necessary.

RECOMMENDATION 6: The GAO recommended that the Secretary of Defense direct the Secretary of the Army to estimate the extent and cost of facility improvements that will be needed at installations scheduled to accommodate the subsequent IBCTs to assist them in their planning.

DoD RESPONSE: Partially concur. The Army routinely conducts estimates as part of the annual Program Objective Memorandum build process. It has developed a draft Transformation Template for Installations (TT-I) to provide Army Major Commands and installations with a menu of facility requirements to support IBCT stationing, training, and sustainment. This template provides a start point for installation planners to determine their facility shortfalls and develop an initial list of required projects to support an IBCT. Accordingly, no further direction to the Army is necessary.

The United States Army Europe (USAREUR) currently is working with DA Staff to determine costs associated with stationing an IBCT in Europe. A visit by Army Staff to USAREUR is tentatively scheduled for early May 02.

RECOMMENDATION 7: The GAO recommended that the Secretary of Defense direct the Secretary of the Army to establish a BCC-type organization at subsequent IBCT locations to deal with day-to-day challenges.

Appendix II
Comments from the Department of Defense

DoD RESPONSE: Partially concur. The Army has identified certain functions, processes, and support capabilities required to transform a unit into an IBCT. Each IBCT location will have different levels of internal staff capability to execute transformation, and the Army will tailor, on a case-by-case basis, the resources required to fill the shortfalls at each location. Lessons learned from Ft. Lewis can be passed on to the subsequent IBCT locations and current BCC function can be executed by a much smaller cell. **Request change to recommendation from "establish" to read "consider."**

RECOMMENDATION 8: The GAO recommended that the Secretary of Defense direct the Secretary of the Army to provide a central collection point for IBCT lessons learned so as to make the information available to personnel throughout the Army.

DoD RESPONSE: Partially concur. The GAO report emphasizes that there is a lack of captured lessons learned on transforming the initial brigades at Fort Lewis. Army Forces Command hosted an Information Exchange Conference at Fort Lewis on 27-29 November 2001 in which lessons learned were briefed to Headquarters Department of the Army, Training and Doctrine Command, Army Materiel Command, and IBCT gaining Major Commands. These lessons learned were not disseminated Army-wide to review or sent to the Center for Army Lessons Learned (CALL). The Army already is planning to establish procedures and a central repository to allow past and future lessons learned to inform Army Transformation. No further direction to the Army is necessary.

GAO's Mission	The General Accounting Office, the investigative arm of Congress, exists to support Congress in meeting its constitutional responsibilities and to help improve the performance and accountability of the federal government for the American people. GAO examines the use of public funds; evaluates federal programs and policies; and provides analyses, recommendations, and other assistance to help Congress make informed oversight, policy, and funding decisions. GAO's commitment to good government is reflected in its core values of accountability, integrity, and reliability.
Obtaining Copies of GAO Reports and Testimony	The fastest and easiest way to obtain copies of GAO documents at no cost is through the Internet. GAO's Web site (www.gao.gov) contains abstracts and full-text files of current reports and testimony and an expanding archive of older products. The Web site features a search engine to help you locate documents using key words and phrases. You can print these documents in their entirety, including charts and other graphics. Each day, GAO issues a list of newly released reports, testimony, and correspondence. GAO posts this list, known as "Today's Reports," on its Web site daily. The list contains links to the full-text document files. To have GAO e-mail this list to you every afternoon, go to www.gao.gov and select "Subscribe to daily E-mail alert for newly released products" under the GAO Reports heading.

Order by Mail or Phone	The first copy of each printed report is free. Additional copies are $2 each. A check or money order should be made out to the Superintendent of Documents. GAO also accepts VISA and Mastercard. Orders for 100 or more copies mailed to a single address are discounted 25 percent. Orders should be sent to:
	
	U.S. General Accounting Office
	441 G Street NW, Room LM
	Washington, D.C. 20548
	
	To order by Phone: Voice: (202) 512-6000
	                                TDD: (202) 512-2537
	                                  Fax: (202) 512-6061

To Report Fraud, Waste, and Abuse in Federal Programs	Contact: Web site: www.gao.gov/fraudnet/fraudnet.htm E-mail: fraudnet@gao.gov Automated answering system: (800) 424-5454 or (202) 512-7470
Public Affairs	Jeff Nelligan, managing director, NelliganJ@gao.gov (202) 512-4800 U.S. General Accounting Office, 441 G Street NW, Room 7149 Washington, D.C. 20548

United States
General Accounting Office
Washington, D.C. 20548-0001

Official Business
Penalty for Private Use $300

Address Service Requested

Presorted Standard
Postage & Fees Paid
GAO
Permit No. GI00

CPSIA information can be obtained at www.ICGtesting.com
Printed in the USA
LVOW09s1225281214

420646LV00017B/421/P